The Cabin

Building a Family-of-Affinity Office

Myra Salzer

ISBN: 0615984207
ISBN 13: 978-0615984209
Library of Congress Control Number: 2014907652
Publisher: Legacy Publications, LLC
Boulder, CO

Contents

.

CHAPTER ONE

Redefining What's Possible

• • •

My career has been all about working with people whose wealth is inherited, people who don't acquire their financial resources through their own creation. Inevitably, the inheritance comes tied to a set of rules (usually in the form of trusts) and values (often to be passed down for generations) and structures (frequently in the form of a family office). In every case, the wealth creator has had some say in how the money is managed, governed, spent, invested, controlled, doled out, given away, or enjoyed. And in every case, those rules, values, and structures—for which the family office becomes the arbiter—result sooner or later in limitations and roadblocks that constrict the heirs' choices.

My clients wouldn't seek the services of The Wealth Conservancy (TWC) if they believed there was an appropriate balance in the manner in which their funds were managed, governed, spent, invested, controlled, doled out, given away, and enjoyed, so I plead guilty to having a skewed perspective on how family offices work. I must admit, my perspective is that family offices, for the most part, create an environment that doesn't serve the well-being of future generations.

There's got to be a better way. And there is. Based on what I've learned from my clients' experiences and having had the good fortune of working with Paul and George (whom you'll read more about throughout this book) and having guidance from countless others, we've designed what we anticipate will be a functional family-of-affinity office. It's called The Cabin, and it exists to serve a group of investors who expect to receive a huge simultaneous distribution. *The Cabin: Building a Family-of-Affinity Office* was prepared to help inheritors who find themselves stuck in structures that don't meet their needs. In designing The Cabin, I've learned the possibilities offered by an alternative family-office structure, and I've guided clients in how to work with their family office to shift the culture of or relationship with their office. These concepts have opened doors for them, and for us. We got clear that The Cabin's focus will be on the individual, not the nuclear family. If we serve only three members of an eight-member family, that's fine. We won't require all or none. If you're an heir with unyielding structures in place, may *The Cabin: Building a Family-of-Affinity Office* open doors for you. If you're a wealth creator in the process of forming a family office, allow this book to help you see possibilities for your family's structure and how you can contribute to generations of joyful wealth. If you're an executive or administrator working for a family office, consider the benefit that might result from shifting your orientation—even a little—toward serving the family members instead of serving the family office. What a difference you could make.

Though the story we tell in *The Cabin* is true, I've taken the liberty of embellishing conversations, names, and circumstances not only to protect individuals who want to remain anonymous but also to present the facts as concisely as possible. My goal is to help you see broader possibilities. May you all find joy.

CHAPTER TWO

Preparing the Blueprints

• • •

One spring evening in 2010, I stopped at the neighborhood market on my way home from work and ran into George, an old acquaintance I had worked with in the '80s. I hadn't seen him since then. He was with his preadolescent daughters, and he had a quixotic glow about him. He asked me if I was still in the business of financial planning, and I was more than a little suspicious when he said he was expecting to come into a great deal of money soon. I said I was and he told me he would call me soon to set up an appointment. As we finished in the produce aisle, I suspected that the chances of him following up with me were slim to none.

Later that week, he called me at the office to make an appointment to see me, but in truth I wasn't eager to spend much time with him. After all, I work with inheritors, and if memory of his family served me correctly, he didn't have that potential. Reinforcing my feeling that he wasn't in line for an inheritance was the fact that he wanted to bring along his friend Paul, "who was also expecting to receive a big windfall." Coincidentally, at the time George and

I met at the grocery store, Paul was researching financial advisory firms to interview. He had heard about The Wealth Conservancy (TWC) from two reliable sources. Not only did George and Paul want to meet with me, the financial planner; they asked to meet with my business partner, Steve Henningsen, as well, who oversees the investment side of our firm.

I agreed to a one o'clock meeting that day, only because I didn't want to offend an old friend. Paul showed up in his signature T-shirt and jeans, George in Keens and shorts, a perfect fit for Steve's crumpled, sockless uniform. To my surprise, as two o'clock rolled around, we were just getting started. The confluence of interests and perspectives resulted in synergies of creativity. It was fun to witness. Paul and George didn't leave TWC until five o'clock and not without putting a follow-up meeting on the calendar.

As it turned out, George, Paul, and more than one hundred of their friends and family had invested in a company—let's call it Northville, Inc.—that has developed technology that has the potential to change the world as dramatically as the invention of the microchip. The expectation was that every investor would simultaneously receive a sizeable dividend as early as the end of 2010, and they wanted TWC to help the investors prepare to "park," and ultimately invest the proceeds. We met regularly over the next several months to help prepare for this most unusual liquidity event. We were talking *big* bucks and Paul and George thought it might be necessary for TWC to prepare itself by hiring one or two additional administrative types. Yeah, right, I thought, and the Tooth Fairy was among the investors and I'm Wonder Woman.

Through our ongoing discussions, I realized that Paul and George's intention in approaching TWC came from caring greatly for their friends and families and for the planet as a whole. They had already formed a private foundation (so they could make a positive difference in the world as soon as possible), and many asset protection trusts were in place. Educational sessions had already been given as well, but the education had been piecemeal, fragmented, and focused primarily on legal structures. I was deeply affected by Paul's commitment to education and particularly to bringing Marshall Rosenberg's nonviolent (compassionate) communication (NVC) techniques into the family-office culture for both client members and staff. NVC is based on the idea that all human beings have the capacity for compassion and resort to violence or behavior that harms others only when they don't recognize more effective strategies for meeting their own needs. Habits of thinking and speaking that lead to the use of violence (psychological and physical) are inherited generationally through culture (including language design itself). NVC assumes all human behavior stems from attempts to meet universal human needs and that these needs are never in conflict. Rather, conflict arises when strategies for meeting those needs clash. NVC proposes that if people can identify their needs, the needs of others, and the feelings that surround those needs, new strategies that meet everyone's needs can be employed successfully.

My vision for the kind of office we might create grew with each meeting we had. I thought about the possibilities every morning as I went for a run and every time I meditated. Ideas even showed up in my dreams at night. The understanding that we would have "unlimited" funds to invest in this family office was freeing. Imagine it! I had the luxury to dream up whatever I could *without financial constraints!* I could envision a structure that would truly serve its members, both internal (staff) and external (investors). We would be a multifamily office, but we wouldn't have a profit motive or a growth imperative.

Paul and George were just as excited as I was. They must have had the little Northville voice singing in their conscious and subconscious minds, because every time we met we had new material and ideas to compile and sort. The possibilities and energy were contagious and the team was formed, indelibly, without the need for contracts or guarantees. It was magical. I couldn't wait to meet with them again.

Of course, Paul and George had the family-and-friend perspective. Mine was an industry perspective. Imagine how liberating it would be for financial planners to be free to spend their time being financial planners without being graded on how many new clients are brought into the firm. If you were a receptionist or an operations manager for such a planning firm, wouldn't you have enormous confidence in just being allowed to do your job? You could build long-term relationships and implement long-term programs knowing you would be there to see the results. After all, the firm would be created so that it would never be sold or swallowed up by another financial institution. If you were a client member (that is, a Northville investor who had benefited from the liquidity event and joined The Cabin), wouldn't you find comfort in knowing that your fees covered only the cost of services rendered without having to wonder about whether the firm's desire for profit is negatively affecting you? And wouldn't it be comforting to know that there was no pressure to sign up for additional, unwanted services? If you were an employee (that is, a staff member), wouldn't you feel valued if you were well paid and were offered healthy meals, workout breaks, and sabbaticals?

Before long we started calling our idea *The Cabin*. It felt safe and did not advertise who we were, whom we served, or why our services were needed. Soon after we gave it a name, George, Paul, and I agreed on its primary purposes, or core values: safety, privacy, and community. If these core values were aligned with the values of the Northville investors, then they would be drawn to join The Cabin community.

Establishing the Principles / Safety, Privacy, Community

Safety relates not only to physical safety but also to safety from judgment. Investors will experience big changes in their lives if the liquidity event happens, and each will experience and process these changes in his own way. It's well documented that when people experience a "sudden money" event such as winning the lottery, they jeopardize their future financial security by making uneducated, irrevocable decisions before they've integrated with their new circumstances. The Cabin will allow client members to process their experiences without harming themselves or others. Staff members will be trained to give their clients the latitude to make choices without being judged, all the while guiding them toward positive long-term decisions.

Privacy is paramount to the vision of The Cabin. We desire to create a haven where internal and external members can be candid without fear, where there are no paparazzi hovering or aggrandizers at the door. We will be stealth, under-the-radar, with no signs on our doors, no numbers listed, no Tweets, no pledged contributions or sponsorships. Like cellophane, we'll be invisible, transparent. Client members and employees who "enjoy the stage"—that is, running for office, being in the news—or whose self-esteem requires status and position to puff it up will be accommodated in ways that don't interfere with the privacy preferred by other members. Security and "un-spin" will be very important elements of the services we provide.

Community, the third core value, will be offered, though not as a prerequisite to becoming a client member of The Cabin. We recognize that the need and desire for community will vary among client members and for each individual over time. This is true for staff members as well. There will be a common element among all of us. We will all be experiencing enormous changes in our lives. The financial circumstances of client members will change dramatically, and those changes could trigger big changes in their personal lives, including new homes, divorces, changes of employment, and entrepreneurial endeavors. The staff may change jobs, and many will be moving to Boulder, Colorado, for work. Everyone will be swimming in what performance coach Kristin Keffeler calls "the caldron of chaos."

George didn't think that suddenly becoming a billionaire would change him. We lovingly teased him about his naïveté. He expected to stay in the same house and maybe do some remodeling, travel as before but perhaps with a newer car or to more exotic places; to shop at the same stores but maybe not make a beeline to the day-old bargains. Having no frame of reference for what huge wealth could mean, he couldn't imagine what his experience might be. The Cabin community will provide a safe environment to explore and experiment with "the new George."

The Cabin will offer community through education programs, social gatherings, vacation spots, camps for children, private web/social community, philanthropic activities, and more. Many client members will want to take advantage of some of the offerings, and The Cabin will be there for them if they choose.

Kismet brought George and Paul to me. Even though I had no family-office experience, my firm was already working on the family-of-affinity office concept and I had a keen understanding of the profound effect a financial windfall could have on someone, especially when the beneficiary of the windfall has done little or nothing to bring it about and has no control over its timing or magnitude. I understood the potential disconnect between net worth and self-worth and the self-destructive behaviors that can result.

Setting the Ground Rules

Having worked with family members who had nothing to do with the formation of their family office, I also understood that family offices don't always nurture family members. The three of us developed a vision of how things could be done differently. Having witnessed what doesn't work, we envisioned a new system of operation. Here are some of the prerequisites:

- Client members must have the option to leave.

- The work environment will be lively and fun.

- The Cabin may cease to exist if it doesn't perform, but it will never be sold.

- The Cabin will not have a profit motive.

- Employees will be well compensated and empowered.

- Only investors of Northville and existing TWC clients will qualify to join The Cabin, and employees will be educated to encourage successfully participating members.

Let's look at each of these prerequisites more closely.

Client Members Must Have the Option to Leave

If you're not a member of a family that has a single-family office, you might be scratching your head at this requirement. Why wouldn't members have the option to leave a family office? Unfortunately, it can happen, and it does. For example, a trust may have been set up from which the member receives income for life, and the trustee may be the family office or an employee of the family office. An heir could inherit a fraction of an illiquid partnership, holding company, or privately held operating business. When family members don't have the option to leave, the management of the family office has less incentive to perform. The family member is trapped and powerless—a structure less likely to nurture self-esteem.

Work Environment Will Be Lively and Fun, Stimulating, and Balanced

You can tell a lot about the effectiveness of a family office by walking in and meeting its employees. One of my clients won't walk into his own family office because "it's too depressing." I wonder how the employees feel about that and how lively and engaged they are. I suspect you don't hear much laughter. The Cabin will exist to serve its family-of-affinity members. Staff members will want to be there, be stimulated by being there, and have fun being there. We'll encourage employees to live balanced lives. We'll offer an environment of continuous learning. For example, at TWC, we're free to schedule a midday workout at the gym, take lengthy vacations, and enjoy a one-month sabbatical every few years. We offer employees occasional reflexology sessions and car-detailing services, among other perks, and we have a comfortable dress code (jeans and shorts are okay, sloppiness isn't). The Cabin will add to that. We envision offering farm-to-table, healthy, balanced breakfasts and lunches, carpooling services, and dry-cleaning pickups. The goal is to create an environment where staff members are free to serve without the usual distractions of daily personal chores.

The Cabin May Cease to Exist If It Doesn't Perform, But It Will Never Be Sold

Single-family offices seem to take on a life of their own, especially a couple generations after the founders pass. The goal becomes growing the assets. I recently attended a meeting with a client and two executives from his family office, and I asked one of the executives what the goal of the family office was. He said, "We want to be around another hundred years—if only the family members wouldn't spend so much!" This tongue-in-cheek response was very telling: Damn the family members for having the audacity to enjoy the life they can afford. The Cabin will exist to serve the needs and wants of each member—judgment free. If the members want to build assets to provide for future generations, that's fine. If they want to give it all away or spend it all during their lifetimes, that's fine as well.

The "it will never be sold" rule enables management and staff to focus on providing superior service rather than building equity value by bringing as many families/assets under management as possible. Increasing The Cabin's book value will not be an objective. A goal like that would be completely counter to creating a safe and fun environment for staff members. Staff performance will not be measured by the number of new families they bring in. That would hardly be the kind of reward that garners loyalty!

That's why The Cabin will never be sold. End of story.

The Cabin Will Not Have a Profit Motive

From an investor-member perspective, profit has a different set of positive ramifications. When you invest with a company, be it a multi-family office or a Goldman Sachs, you know its goal is to charge you as much as it can and yet keep you happy enough not to leave. So the investor's goal becomes finding a way to get more for less, while the company's goal is to give less and charge more. Sometimes the investor comes out on top, sometimes not. The relationship takes energy. You continually question it and negotiate the cost. The Cabin, however, will charge each client member on a pro rata basis, plus the actual cost of the individual services used. Its goal will be to serve at the level the client member wants, and the member will decide how much service is desired. The cost to provide superior services in the absence of a profit motive will yield a very reasonable expense of membership.

Employees Will Be Well Compensated and Will Feel Empowered
I want The Cabin to be the most sought-after financial-services employer on the planet. If we create an attractive work environment, we will attract the most appropriate employees culled from the best of the best. The appeal of an ideal workplace where employees feel empowered will be enhanced by high wages and comprehensive benefits.

At TWC, we use a filter for "grading" clients. (My entrepreneurial coach, Dan Sullivan, of Strategic Coach, Inc. inspired this filter.) We grade clients on a scale of 1-5 in five areas:

1. Is our expertise a good fit for the client's needs?

2. Does the client's circumstances offer an opportunity to expand our expertise?

3. How much revenue does the client generate?

4. How often does the client refer us to others or provide references to prospective clients?

5. Is the client fun or enjoyable to work with? How much appreciation is shown for our services?

Anyone at TWC, no matter his/her position, may terminate a client who doesn't score 15 or higher. This happens *very* rarely. Just knowing that the tool is there and that they have control over their work environment empowers employees.

The Cabin will have a similar filter, although points 3 and 4 will be different, because we won't have a profit motive or a reason to bring in additional members. I believe the ability to grade clients is even more important in The Cabin environment because client members might assume a sense of entitlement because they're "members." This will not be the case; they'll earn their membership.

Only Shareholders of Northville (and Their Heirs) Will Qualify to Join The Cabin. There will be one exception to this rule: Clients of TWC will be invited to continue working with us.

CHAPTER THREE

The Cabin Takes Shape

• • •

Without any preconceived ideas in mind, we wanted to convey our ideas graphically. I started drawing ovals and rectangles, and Paul and George used the initial diagram to expand. Over time, The Cabin took form. The three of us met regularly, though in our initial meetings, we had no idea how far we would go. I learned a little about the investors, most of whom have connections to Paul as friends and family. The investors are not easily categorized in terms of the number of shares owned, their ages, geography, lifestyle, or experience with financial wealth. The only common denominator I saw, besides their connection to Paul, was the willingness to invest in a technology that would make the world a better place.

There are more than one hundred investors overall in Paul's circle. The number of shares each owns varies from minimal to significant. Most are U.S. citizens and most live in the United States. If the liquidity event happens as the investors expect, their new financial circumstances will bring them all into a new, unfamiliar realm. When the first liquidity event is announced, they may go from being unknown to highly pursued. The Cabin hopes to be able to educate them to enjoy the changes, while helping steer them clear of those with undesirable agendas.

The Structure of The Cabin

One of the first objectives of The Cabin will be to provide a place for client members to park their funds. This will give them time to integrate with their new circumstances and provide them the luxury of what author Susan Bradley, a former financial planner and founder of the Sudden Money Institute, coined the "decision-free zone"—or the DFZ, as we affectionately refer to it. While the client members remain in the DFZ, we'll be building a firm whose structure accommodates their needs. Figure 1, below, illustrates the structure of The Cabin.

Figure 1: The Cabin Structure

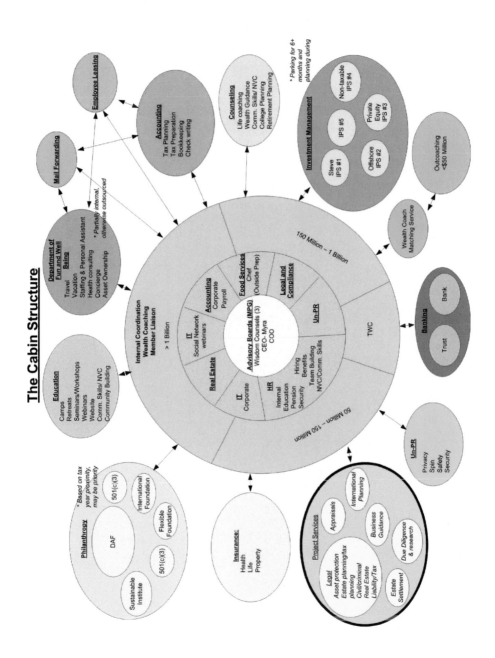

The Experience of The Cabin

The client members will experience a relationship with a team of wealth coaches and member liaisons including certified financial planners and attorneys, coaches, and paraplanners; all of varying backgrounds. These contact persons will grow intimately familiar with the client members individually and will help them assess which of the numerous services will be appropriate and best for them. Some client members may take advantage of every service (see ovals in Figure 2); others, only one or two. We intend to make the Department of Education, the Department of Fun (DOF), and the Department of Counseling available to everyone as soon as possible. The other departments may take years to develop, as will some of the back-office functions (see rectangles in Figure 2), which would be invisible to the client members but prerequisites to offering services. Figure 2 illustrates how the client members will experience The Cabin.

Figure 2: The Cabin Experience

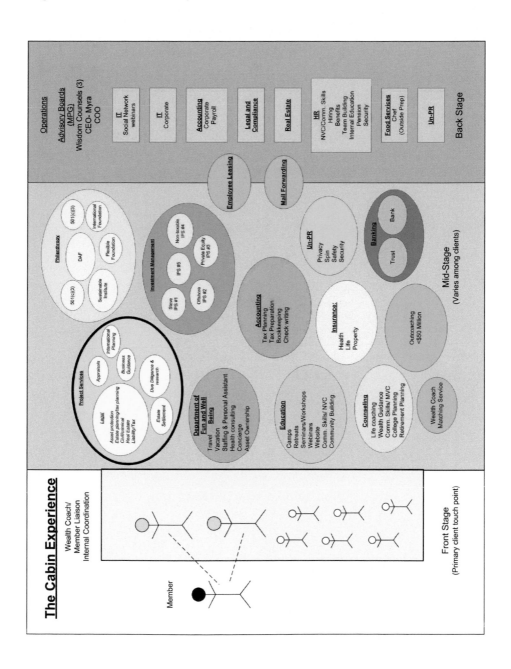

For a typical single and multi-family office, the family is the client; for The Cabin, the individual member is the client. Individual choice is one of the biggest advantages that distinguish The Cabin from single-family and multi-family offices. That difference is critical because things can change. Two generations from the founding of the family office, many of the grandchildren may decide to seek additional advisors, or they may not have any assets left, or they may decide to manage everything themselves or hire another firm to do so. The Cabin structure allows for that. The Cabin structure encourages independence, promoting everyone's freedom, rather than inhibiting it. It will provide options and boundaries and give client members choices and opportunities—including the opportunity to thrive and/or fail—with support and without judgment.

The Cabin may be generally permissive, but one value is paramount: each member's right to privacy. Many companies and multi-family offices have a public-relations department to get as much publicity as possible, but we want to be anonymous. Figures 1 and 2 indicate a department of Un-PR, for both staff and members. Privacy—everybody's privacy—will be sacrosanct, including among family members. Wealth coaches for one family member will keep information from all other family members confidential to the extent desired. The Cabin will be a safe haven for every individual who joins, regardless of familial ties.

By the fall of 2010, The Cabin structure had evolved to the inner circle much as it appears in Figure 1, with about 75 percent of the departments surrounding it. At that time, Paul, George, and I thought that a liquidity event was imminent. That possibility was terrifying. Though we were developing a vision for what was possible, we had no clue how to build the structure should that possibility become reality. Paul is an entrepreneur, George is a scientist, and I work with inheritors. None of us has family-office experience. What if the close of the deal was imminent?

My best hope of being prepared was to get the ear of the "Muhammad Ali" of family governance, the "Vito Corleone" of family offices, the "Dali Lama" of the industry, and the architect of the ideal: James E. Hughes, Jr. (Jay), the author of *Family Wealth—Keeping It in the Family: How Family Members and Their Advisers Preserve Human, Intellectual, and Financial Assets for Generations.*

I decided to make the call.

CHAPTER FOUR

To the Mountaintop

• • •

Well, the truth is I sent Jay an email rather than make the call. That way I wouldn't have to hear a rejection. And I didn't mention my plan to Paul and George or copy them on the email because I didn't want them to be discouraged by a rejection, should it arrive. The email went something like this:

From: Myra Salzer
Sent: December 14, 2010 9:53 AM
To: James Hughes
Subject: Expert guidance needed
Attachments: 📄 The Cabin Structure.pdf (18.1 KB)   📄 The Cabin Experience.pdf (18.3 KB)

Dear Jay,

You may remember me. We initially met in the early '90s at Peter White's gathering at the Arlie Conference Center in Virginia. *(I said* that to show I'm in the industry; who else would know about Peter's International Skye's annual conferences?) We also met for breakfast in Aspen a couple years ago (I wasn't at all sure he'd remember that) and you helped a client and me last year with that challenge involving FOX.

Well, the reason I am reaching out to you now is because I need your help (It's always a good idea to be up front when asking a favor of a wise elder). I am working with a couple gentlemen, Paul and George, who have invested in a technology that is likely to result in a historic liquidity event. (If it didn't destroy my credibility, I thought it would at least get his attention.) Many of their friends and family members are also investors. Collectively, they total over a hundred individuals and they could get $billions. In fact, some of them, individually, may become billionaires. The timing and amount(s) are completely out of their control because they are merely shareholders of a privately held, offshore company that has developed a technology that could possibly be a serious game changer. (Oh, dear, another claim that could destroy my credibility.)

We want to build a family-of-affinity office (I thought it wise to let him know I'd read his second book) to help them manage the money that will be coming to them. The two attachments, The Cabin Structure and The Cabin Experience, illustrate the plans we've come up with so far. (We may be wackos, but at least we're crazies with a thoughtful plan.) My vision is to make this financial-services organization optional for the investors, and one that will not have a profit motive. Its sole purpose will be to serve the members who want to be served and to give them options regarding which services they want to take advantage of. I also want to create a peerless work environment, where we can attract the best of the best in all departments.

We are kind of at a loss as to where to go from here, because we need someone well connected in and respected by the industry to point out the next steps we need to take. *(Unimaginative flattery? Guilty as charged.)*

Would you please agree to meet with us? We would be happy to drive up to Aspen and meet with you for as much time as you can spare. Please let me know.

Very warm regards,

Myra Salzer

 THE WEALTH
CONSERVANCY, INC.

*Honoring your worth / Taking
care of your wealth
303-444-1919 / 303-444-1479 fax
www.TWCinc.org*

Never vague, Jay responded with a message that was swift and to the point:

From: James E. Hughes, Jr.
Sent: December 14, 2010 9:58 AM
To: Myra Salzer
Subject: RE: Expert guidance needed

Of course, I remember you, and I'd be happy to meet. Between the holidays and upcoming travel, the earliest I could meet is February 10. I could drive to Rifle and you could fly there *(Clearly, he thought we already had enough money to charter a plane; if only he knew).* That would save you a lot of time.

Namaste,

Jay
James Hughes

From: Myra Salzer (Myra@twcinc.org)
Sent: December 14, 2010 10:22 AM
To: George; Paul
Subject: Expert advice!

Hi, George and Paul,

Do you remember the name Jay Hughes? I gave you copies of his books a few months ago. There is no one on the planet in a better position to guide us *and* he is willing to meet with us and point us in some positive directions. This is a big deal. A really big deal! He lives in Aspen. Believe me, it will be worth the drive. This is really important. Please plan to spend the full day, February 10. We'll probably leave Boulder at about 5:30 a.m. OK?

Myra Salzer

Honoring your worth / Taking care of your wealth
303-444-1919 / 303-444-1479 fax
www.TWCinc.org

From: Paul
Sent: December 14, 2010 10:37 AM
To: Myra Salzer
CC: George
Subject: RE: Expert advice!

Got it! I'm in. :-D
P

From: George
Sent: December 14, 2010 10:42 AM
To: Myra Salzer
CC: Paul
Subject: RE: Expert advice!

I'll have to check with Joanie and see if she can pick up the kids that day. I'll let you know.

George

From: George
Sent: December 15, 2010 8:22 AM
To: Myra Salzer
CC: Paul
Subject: RE: Expert Advice

Myra and Paul,

Were good to go on the 10th.

George

From: Myra Salzer (Myra@twcinc.org)
Sent: December 16, 2010 9:12 AM
To: Jay Hughes
Subject: Feb. 10 meeting

Dear Jay,

Thank you for your kind offer to meet in Rifle. That's very generous of you. The truth is that we need to economize, and driving is our only option. Feb. 10 will work for us and we can leave Boulder by 5:30 a.m., so we should be able to meet in Aspen by 9:30, assuming we aren't slowed by weather. Should we just plan on starting at 10:00? Do you want to decide where to meet now, or wait until after the holidays?

I am so excited and grateful for your offer. Thank you!

Warmly,

Myra Salzer

Honoring your worth / Taking care of your wealth
303-444-1919 / 303-444-1479 fax
www.TWCinc.org

From: James Hughes
Sent: December 16, 2010 9:50 AM
To: Myra Salzer
Subject: RE: Feb. 10 meeting

Dear Myra,

I am honored and look forward to this. Your diagrams are impressive. Let's meet at the Hotel Colorado in Glenwood Springs. That way you won't have to leave quite so early to meet at 10. We can have lunch right there.

Namaste,

Jay
James Hughes

Minutes later, from Myra to Jay, copying Paul and George:

From: Myra Salzer (Myra@twcinc.org)
Sent: December 16, 2010 10:17 AM
To: Jay Hughes
CC: Paul, George
Subject: RE: Feb. 10 meeting

Dear Wonderful Jay,

It's a date! Happy holidays and safe travels. ☺
With joy and gratitude,

Myra Salzer

Honoring your worth / Taking care of your wealth
303-444-1919 / 303-444-1479 fax
www.TWCinc.org

We made our travel arrangements, but before meeting with Jay, I attended a Northville shareholder meeting. Paul, his wife, other investors in his circle, and I flew overseas for the meeting. It was a worthwhile trip because I got to meet and hear from the CEO of the technology company, as well as the chief scientist/developer. Just as important, I got to meet several other investors, many of whom were Americans from other parts of the country. I got a sense of their level of sophistication (not consistently high), their interests (a diverse group), and their connection (a commitment to doing what they could to benefit the planet).

Meeting some of the investors confirmed for me that The Cabin was vital to them and critical to their well-being. Our meeting with Jay only reinforced the necesssity of The Cabin. After surprisingly few and delightfully concise additional emails, Paul, George, and Melissa Hoyer (a certified financial planner (CFP®) and Certified Professional Co-Active Coach at TWC, who could record meetings far better than the three of us) drove to the mountaintop—well, as far up as Glenwood Springs at least—to meet with Jay. It was magical.

The historic Hotel Colorado, which sits by natural spring pools, is a grand building off I-70, about an hour north of Aspen. It has a quiet elegance of days gone by, not difficult to find in Europe or even on the East Coast but relatively rare in the West. We settled into a quiet corner of the restaurant, the only guests.

Before we even got started, before building any kind of connection, Jay, seemingly out of the blue, asked Paul for a dollar. Paul's brow furrowed, but his doubts didn't keep him from producing the bill. Jay responded with his penetrating belly laugh and said, "Thank you. Now you have privilege!" That built instant rapport, and we got down to business. Jay asked direct questions: Who are the investors? What is the nature of the investment? How and when will investors receive funds? Paul answered, with input from George, while Jay listened. Melissa took notes. I knitted (it helps me listen). We got lost in the conversation and forgot to get hungry for lunch until the waiter came by with menus. We talked and we ate and we talked and we talked.

In less than two hours, Jay got the lay of the land. Paul's numerous circle of investors, some of whom had only one or two shares, but one or two shares could be worth hundreds of thousands of dollars. And some of the investors owned thousands of shares. They could become billionnaires. Even those with only a few shares, though, would undoubtedly experience a lifestyle shock. A couple of the investors were unemployed and had been given shares as gifts. Paul knew of one investor who had recently filed for bankruptcy.

Jay listened intently and heard us clearly. Then he spoke, and we listened. Through it all, Melissa took notes. As we listened, our heads began to spin. What had we gotten into? Jay made us realize (or at least start to realize) the magnitude of the journey we had begun. We weren't building The Cabin as an asset-management firm. The Cabin would be a souls-under-management firm. I doubted I was ready for that.

Jay reassured us that nobody on the planet could be better suited to the challenge. After all, these investors will be more like inheritors than wealth creators; they will likely receive a sum of money, the timing of which is out of their control. What's more, it will be an amount disproportionate to their earning ability. It will be life changing.

Jay explained that even with positive life changes, people experience a mourning process. They mourn the loss of the life they knew. They mourn the loss of friendships that might never be the same. They mourn the loss of having to struggle financially. They mourn the loss of needing to work, of needing to stay married, of needing to get good grades, of needing to fix things themselves, of needing to search for bargains, of knowing their friends are with them because they're truly friends and not because they have money. Most of all, they mourn the loss of simplicity.

Singer-songwriter Kris Kristofferson (and Fred Foster) wrote, "Freedom's just another word for nothing left to lose." The Cabin investors may never be free again. They may decide they need to spend time learning about investments, estate planning, philanthropy, taxes, teaching their children a work ethic, hiring and firing, privacy, estate settlement, and a myriad of other components of wealth. The Cabin will be their safety net, where they can be themselves, be understood, and learn as much as they *choose* to.

There was silence in the car driving home.

CHAPTER FIVE

A Focus on Well-Being

• • •

Paul, George, Melissa, and I met the following Monday to debrief and plan. Our heads were no longer spinning, but our hearts were. The synchronicity we experienced was magical.

We were perfectly clear about what we didn't want: ego-driven, asset accumulation, and control lasting the next five hundred years. We wanted to promote individualism and freedom among client members. I've seen too often how a family office and its well-being can become the focus of an operation instead of the family members and their well-being. The driven, controlling creator of the wealth often structures his family office the same way he did his business, but what succeeds in a business does not always translate to what's best for a family. Family members can't be treated like employees, with "salaries," "benefits," and limited "vacation time"—not without unfortunate consequences.

We desired the client members to have the opportunity to succeed on their own, within The Cabin's boundaries and beyond. And we wanted Northville investors to have the freedom to fail as well, which is equally important. How else will they learn to thrive?

With this in mind, we concluded that The Cabin's value proposition would be to prize, above all else, its members' and employees' *safety* and *privacy* and offer *community* to the extent desired by each individual. These priorities laid the perfect foundation for discussing how The Cabin would be structured.

Larger family-office structures are usually somewhat linear, hierarchal, and bureaucratic, similar to what's outlined in Figure 3.

Figure 3: A Structure of a Larger Family Office

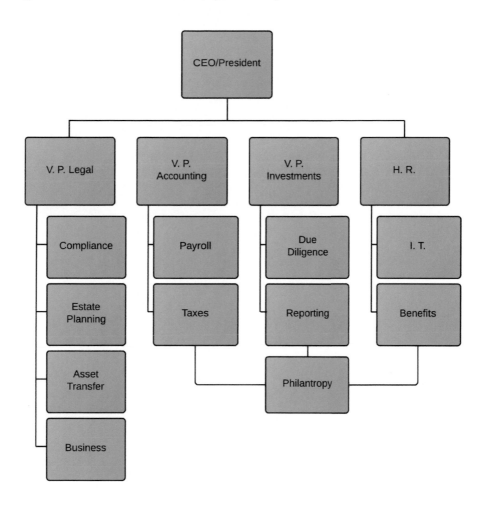

The Cabin has a circular structure (see Figure 4, The Cabin Structure). No one is at the top—especially not a CEO—or the bottom. Some of The Wealth Conservancy's clients also happen to be members of family offices with autocratic, unapproachable CEOs. I didn't want the Northville investors or their progeny to experience anything like that. I envisioned The Cabin as a nourishing refuge for Northville investors and The Cabin employees alike. No CEO was going to dominate it. I envisioned building an organization where faultfinding was nonexistent. There would be no hierarchal, finger-pointing bosses saying, "Hey, you, do this," or "Hey, you, do that." If no one at the top pointed fingers, no one in a "lower" position would have to point a finger at someone else and say, "Not my fault! He told me to do it."

Figure 4: The Cabin Structure

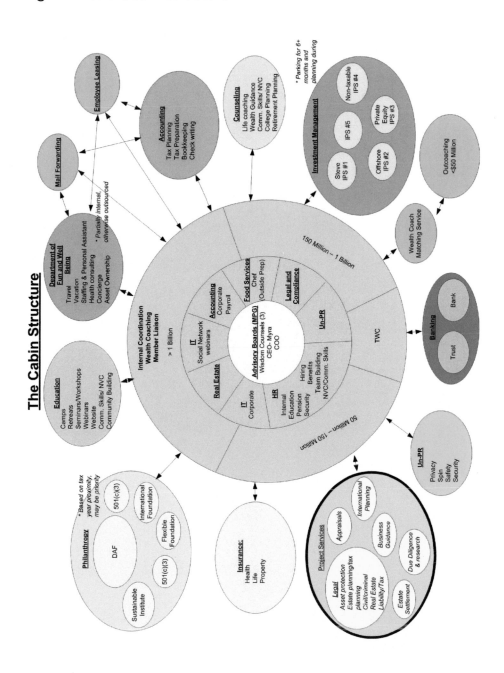

Every circle in The Cabin structure has a purpose. There is no competition among the departments and services, each being self-supporting and not created to make a profit or be measured by a total market.

Some family offices are organized so that the family member's experience, two generations after the wealth creator is gone, is one that allows very little interaction (see Figure 5).

Figure 5. The Family Member's Place in the Family Office

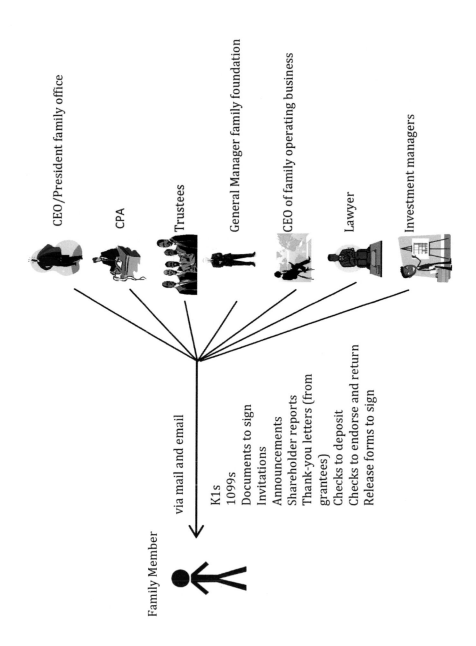

Notice the monodirectional relationship among the advisors and fiduciaries. In my experience, it's rare to see a healthy exchange in which the family office invites input from the family member/beneficiary. I once heard a fiduciary/trustee lament how much easier his job would be if only the beneficiary were in a coma! How can an heir be expected to develop high self-esteem and confidence in such an environment?

Figure 6, The Cabin Experience, captures how The Cabin's family members will experience their family-of-affinity office. Each client member will have a team of wealth coaches and member liaisons to offer a sense of perspective. These teams will coordinate as needed among the departments, including the Departments of Education, Counseling, Project Services, Accounting, Philanthropy, etc. It will not be necessary for family members to navigate the waters of investments alone—unless they want to. In other words, if family members want to choose their own managers or directly choose their own investments, they will be free to do so. If the same family members want to delegate the management of their charitable giving, however, there will be resources for them to do so, all coordinated by their wealth-coaching team.

Figure 6: The Cabin Experience

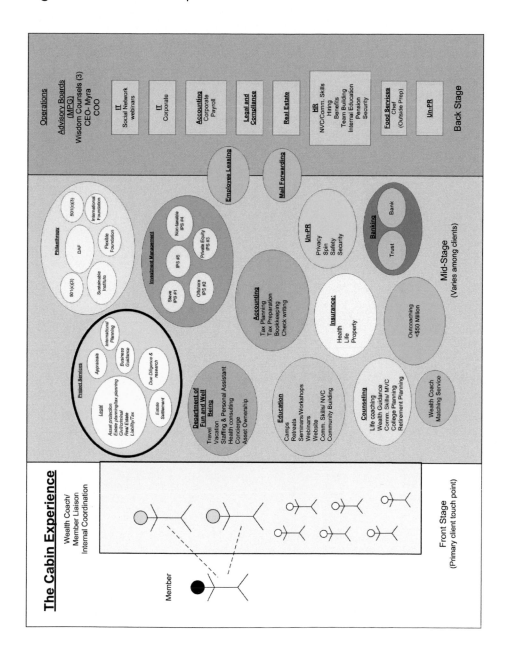

Such flexibility is not necessarily the case in many family offices. Instead, there can be distance and alienation. That's how things have been for a client I'll call Dana. She's a twenty-six-year-old, fourth-generation family member served by a typically structured family office. Her great-grandfather spearheaded what is now a multinational ad agency. She doesn't know much about the business, and, in fact, neither do her siblings or cousins. Her grandfather is the current CEO of the company and has not indicated he has any interest in retiring *ever*. He is too busy running the company to attend family meetings. Most of the family resides on the East Coast, but before Dana was born, her mother "escaped" West, where she felt she could be anonymous. Dana's mother resented the role that her father inherited and resented how her own half-siblings and step-siblings seemed to have a closer relationship with the family office than she did.

When Dana turned twenty-five, she started to receive monthly checks from the family office's trust company. She isn't sure why or how long they will continue, and she has no idea whom to ask—certainly not her mother. No one at the family office had ever reached out to her, introduced himself, offered to educate, listen, lend a hand, or even, for that matter, interact with her until a few months earlier. The assistant to the CFO at the family office asked for Dana's bank information, saying, "It would be so much easier if the funds were automatically wired into your account so I don't have to manually write a check every month."

There is a disconnect between Dana's monthly deposits and the rest of her life. She has many questions. Dana's mother stopped going to the family-office meetings years ago, and Dana sensed that if she tried to attend any, her mother would construe it as an act of disloyalty toward her. Now that Dana is a certified physical therapist after seven years at California State University-Northridge and the University of Southern California, she feels caught in limbo, not knowing if she can afford to work part time or rent a house without roommates. Or if she even wants to! She already felt disenfranchised among her peers because she never had to get student loans and graduated debt free. If that wasn't embarrassing enough, her graduation gift was a new A4 Audi.

Dana's experience isn't unique. A little education about her wealth would go a long way. The need for it seems so obvious, so simple. But everyone at the family office is very, very busy. They have money to move, invest, protect, and save taxes on. They do a good job for the family office, and that's the point I'm making: Family office employees work for the family office, not for the family members.

The Cabin will be different. Family members will be the heart of the organization. Family members will have options for using the services available so that they may take advantage of those that interest them and pass on those that don't. Paul, George, and I want to make education available to all, and that work has already begun. Paul has been studying Marshall Rosenberg's nonviolent communication (NVC) techniques for many years, and he wants to make the techniques available to all investors and employees and to draw from many ideas and techniques including Nancy Kline's, the Sudden Money Institute, learning styles, permaculture, the Cauldron of Chaos, among others. Even though no distributions have been made, The Cabin has offered members several education programs. Though the goal has been to learn and to prepare for a future distribution, the process has resulted in building a community now.

CHAPTER SIX

The Cabin Services: A Closer Look

• • •

The Cabin will offer a wide range of services (see Figure 7), but the core services will be wealth coaching and transition, that is, financial and life planning with compassion. Each client member will have a team of wealth coaches and liaisons working on his or her behalf. This team is likely to be two to five financial planners with complementary skills, strengths, learning styles, and expertise. Different areas of expertise might include financial planning, accounting, law, investments, and coaching/counseling. Client members will benefit from the team approach because they should always be able to contact at least one advisor on their team who knows them and their unique circumstances.

The team will be chosen to complement each of their clients. Learning styles—auditory, visual, or kinesthetic—play an important role in educating clients because styles vary among individuals (both staff and members). Showing a lot of pictures to an auditory learner, for example, won't get you very far. Jay Hughes has emphasized how important it is to understand a client's learning style and has resourced consultants who will work with us on identifying those styles.

Figure 7: The Cabin Structure

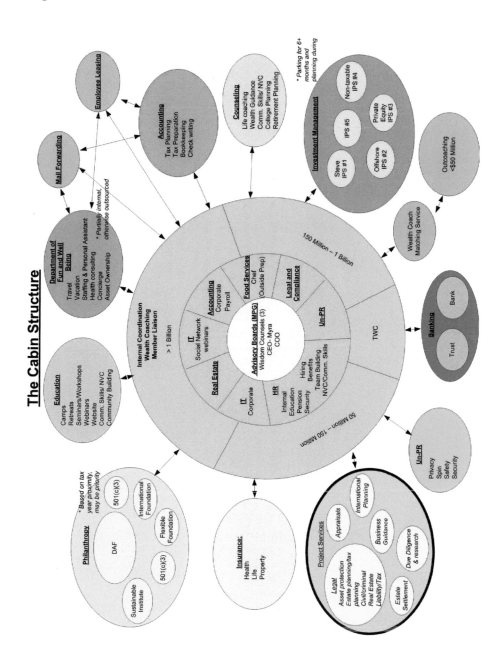

In Figure 7, the center circle indicates four separate membership classifications, three defined by levels of wealth and one identified as some of The Wealth Conservancy's clients. The classifications are grouped according to allocation and expertise. The expertise needed to coaching a billionaire member is different from what's needed for a fifty-million-dollar member. The complexity of a client's circumstances also affects the expertise needed on the wealth-coaching team. The Cabin's financial projections assumed a team of five wealth coaches per client member at the high end of the financial spectrum and a team of three wealth coaches per five client members whose wealth ranges from $50 million to $150 million.

The wealth coaches will be familiar with each of the services offered in their domain. That means being generalists, not specialists. It would be impossible and undesirable for any one person to be expert in all the areas we plan to serve.

Education

Education is the service to which George, Paul, and I are most committed. We plan to offer online and on-site sessions on technical topics, such as tax law, and general life topics, such as communications, and to make the sessions available to as many Northville shareholders as possible (whether Cabin clients or not). We want to offer shareholders, their children, and grandchildren money camps and excursions designed for them. Paul made some education sessions available to Northville shareholders even before we began working together on The Cabin.

In the pro forma, we budgeted for media/training staff to record and memorialize the numerous in-house and outsourced educational sessions we intend to provide. This will enable Northville client members to view sessions on their own schedule. Those who attend the sessions in person will benefit from the community component as well. The excursions will be even more effective at community building. Members will have control over their degree of Involvement.

Among the communications topics we'll introduce both to Cabin staff and to Northville client members is nonviolent communication and Nancy Kline's Time-to-Think methodology.

Just when we started to build confidence in the direction we were headed, Jay matter-of-factly pointed out that subject-based education doesn't work. That was a surprise to us. Thanks to Jay, we now understand that before we can provide a lesson on tax law, for example, we'll need to do assessments on everyone involved and build skills in the areas discussed below. These assessments are in development with people far better equipped to describe them than I, so I will merely touch on each category and let you explore the implications as they apply to your family office.

Fun and Well-Being

Anything related to enjoyment, fulfillment, and fun will be the business of the Department of Fun and Well-Being. Its services will be offered to all Northville client members as soon as possible. We envision these services as being offered adjunct, pay-as-you-go, and expect members with greater financial resources to take the greatest advantage of them. This department will manage vacations and vacation homes, provide concierge services, help with hiring household staff, match members with college consultants, oversee the organization of family reunions, plan parties, book yoga retreats, and whatever else a member can afford to dream up.

In line with the three core values of The Cabin, the Department of Fun and Well-Being will also address issues of safety, privacy, and community.

Investment Management

Steve Henningsen, who heads The Wealth Conservancy's Investment Department, will be The Cabin's go-to person after a liquidity event. His first priority will be to make it possible for all Northville client members to park their funds in a safe place while they're in their DFZ (decision-free zone). The Counseling group will explain this in detail. Beyond that, Steve will focus on bringing in managers of investment managers so that he can return to spending his time on his passion—analyzing economics, managing investment policy, and finding managers who can provide the piece of the portfolio to fit the policy.

Wealth coaches will work with the client members and the Investment Management Department in conjunction with the Accounting Department to determine the appropriateness of holding domestic/foreign/offshore/private equity/nontaxable assets in client members' portfolios. This department will also be responsible for composite performance reporting and communicating with accountants about any investments having tax consequences.

One of the beauties of our vision is that there will be no financial incentive to manage members' funds. If a member isn't aligned with our approach, s/he will be invited to use other firms for investment-management services. That action will not preclude a member from enjoying other services The Cabin will offer. Though this arrangement may not seem like a big deal, it differs greatly from the typical multifamily office, where there is a profit incentive to increase assets under management and pressure on the staff to bring in more clients with more assets. We believe we will be able to attract quality wealth coaches who want nothing more than to coach and to serve, and have no interest in marketing for their employers.

Philanthropy

When I met Paul and George, I was wowed by their commitment to the betterment of the planet. They had been working on community projects via the Institute for years and had already worked with a couple Northville shareholders in creating private foundations.

The Philanthropy Department staff will work with wealth coaches to determine which types of organizational structures (for example, operating or non-operating private foundation, donor-advised funds, direct contributions to 501(c)(3)s, supporting organizations) are the best fit for Northville client members. If members have a passion to devote time to such endeavors, the wealth coaches and philanthropy specialists will guide them in making good choices. The Philanthropy Department and the Department of Fun and Well-Being might work together to offer volunteer vacation options to members.

Insurance

Members will have a lot of assets to protect, and insurance will be a valuable tool in doing so. We will develop relationships with independent insurers or possibly self-insure, depending on whether it makes sense for client members. Until there is a liquidity event and we know the magnitude and timing of distributions, we can't project the scope of this department.

Banking

We will form our own bank and private trust company (perhaps both domestically and offshore) to provide banking services to Northville shareholder members while protecting their privacy and minimizing expenses. These entities will require as much as a couple of years to form. In the interim, The Cabin members will safely park their funds.

Accounting

We are in communication with Bill Cline, CPA, who is likely to build and manage this department. It will be available to client members who want The Cabin to oversee their check writing, bill paying, tax preparation, and/or education to manage or participate in their own affairs. Systems will be created so that this department will seamlessly communicate with wealth coaches and the Department of Investment Management.

Counseling

Money makes a difference in a person's life. Having it is often a blessing, but even when it changes life for the better, change is indeed involved, and that is often challenging. Most of the Northville shareholders will experience a significant life change if there is a liquidity event. Their financial circumstances will likely be dramatically different, affecting almost all aspects of life, including their relationships, self-esteem, and work. They may never be able to return to their former, "normal" life. That life will be lost to them, and they may need time to mourn that loss. If they don't experience the normal mourning process, if they're in denial, any major decisions they make may be less beneficial.

The Counseling Department will offer guidance not only for client members but also for its employees, all of whom will be experiencing changes. The Cabin staff will experience dramatic changes in their work and personal lives. They will all have new jobs; many will have to relocate. They will encounter new colleagues, procedures, clients, and their financial circumstances will change as well. Smooth adjustment is critical, and we're working with two excellent professionals—psychologist Jim Grubman, Ph.D. and Susan Bradley—to guide us through this process.

Employee Leasing
Employee leasing will make it easy for client members to hire staff without the hassles of managing their own employees. Client members may "lease" some staff members (such as nannies, gardeners, and household help) who technically will be employees of the leasing company. The leasing company will take care of benefits such as medical insurance, vacation pay, unemployment insurance, and pensions. The Northville client member will have to pay only the leasing company. Presto!

Un-PR
The Un-PR Department will honor two of The Cabin's three core values—privacy and safety. We intend to serve this function through education and safe systems. This department will be involved with our internal and member-driven information technology (IT), as well as with security for client members and their families and property. I expect this department will offer education courses so that members can learn how to remain private and fly under the radar.

Mail Forwarding

To maximize members' privacy, security, and freedom, we plan to use an in-house or outsourced mail-forwarding service so that the sender would not know the whereabouts of the Northville client members. We'll scan and upload mail to secure website portals so information can be accessed from anywhere client members have internet connections.

Project Services

Unlike the other departments, whose services will be ongoing, the Project Services Department will oversee one-time or as-needed services. For example, when a relative of a member of The Cabin dies, we'll guide the family through the estate-settlement process, arranging for appraisals as needed, and finding legal counsel in the states of titled property. Many legal services, such as prenuptial agreements and divorces, do not require ongoing follow-up. Estate plans require updates in the event of a change of some sort, such as a tax-law change, a death, or a birth. If a member of The Cabin wants to start a business then we will offer guidance, and if they want to buy a business then we will assist in due diligence to explore its viability. If a member wants to move out of the country, we'll analyze the tax ramifications of doing so.

Outside Wealth-Coach Matching

A number of Northville shareholders will not become members of The Cabin. They may not have enough wealth to justify becoming a member, they may not be aligned with The Cabin's values, they may want to work with another firm, or they may want the added privacy of forming an individual family office. In such cases, we plan to help them find a firm suited to their needs.

Overall

To support the services listed above, The Cabin will need internal departments including IT, human resources, legal, compliance, food service, accounting and payroll, and property management. But what excites me more than anything is the department that's missing: The Cabin will not have a marketing team.

CHAPTER SEVEN

The Employee Experience

• • •

Because The Cabin will provide an ideal workplace experience for employees, it will attract its pick of employees culled from the best of the best. They will be members of an elite group. They won't be the prima donnas of the industry. They will be stealthy, hardworking, service-oriented givers who aren't afraid to put in long hours, when necessary, while laughing and having fun doing so. The atmosphere at the offices will be bright, sunny, open, and joyful. Staff will be relaxed and comfortable yet put together and professional. Informal, yes; sloppy, no.

The same values that apply to client members will apply to its employees and contractors as well—namely, security, privacy, and community. Community will be even more important among employees because of the camaraderie that will naturally evolve as a result of the need to honor the privacy of client members. Truth be told, several of the employees will also be Northville shareholders. I won't be the only one in that category. Several of these people have expressed an interest in working in areas such as wealth coaching, education, philanthropy, legal counsel, and food services.

Speaking of food service, we intend to support a healthy, balanced lifestyle for employees, one that includes farm-to-table (maybe even grown on the property) breakfasts and lunches. We intend to make it easy for employees to get to and from work, so we're likely to offer a shuttle service. We'll encourage them to exercise their bodies as well as their minds with year-round activities including cycling, swimming, running, yoga, palates, and gym workouts. The budget will also accommodate a holistic physician on staff.

At The Wealth Conservancy, salaried employees may take paid free days at their discretion. It has not been an abused benefit and we plan to continue the practice. We anticipate the culture of trust and camaraderie will carry through to The Cabin. TWC employees also get a one-month paid sabbatical every three years. These sabbaticals have proven beneficial not only for the employees but also for the organization. They've encouraged us to cross-train and work in teams so we can cover for one another while someone is on sabbatical. The Cabin employees will be given the same benefits from the start.

Depending on the size of the distributions and the pace at which The Cabin can recruit qualified people, there may likely be anywhere from 100-400 employees. Our pay scales will be above the top range. Most employees will not be given permission to work from their homes, and we won't be able to offer part-time work or extensive flex schedules. We will, however, provide health insurance, a generous retirement benefit, cell phones, and reimbursements for continuing education (both related and unrelated to their work at The Cabin) and relocation expenses.

Security will be tight. Prospective employees will have to agree to thorough background checks. While at work, strict protocols, which will depend on the department and the person's position within it, will enable varying degrees of information access. Compliance with the regulations of the Security and Exchange Commission and the Office of the Comptroller of the Currency will be strictly enforced. Our intention is to work with counsel to give us as much flexibility as possible with the minimum government oversight allowable, and I emphasize *allowable*. We have no incentive to push compliance boundaries, but nonetheless, we want to have as much flexibility as we can.

To start, our offices will operate exclusively in Boulder, Colorado. Once the infrastructure is in place and we've honed the wealth-coaching team systems, we're likely to branch out to Los Angeles and New York, where there are several Northville shareholders.

I want to stress again—because I believe it's such a huge employee benefit—that employees will not be required or expected to bring in more business. Employees needn't worry about the magnitude of the firm's **assets under management.** They need to be concerned only about the **souls under management.** The Cabin's focus will not be on **transactions,** but rather on **transitions and service.** We will form The Cabin with the intention that expenses approximate membership dues. We will not have to run the business with alliances split between members and owners because there won't be any owners outside of The Cabin expecting a share of the profits. In addition, The Cabin will never be sold. We will not be gobbled up by large Wall Street firms or international financial institutions. Employees will never have to worry about that sort of change. Once in, employees will find The Cabin to be a safe haven.

CHAPTER EIGHT

The Cabin's Founding Families and Build-Out

• • •

The Cabin is an exciting and inspiring prospect. It redefines not only the scope of services that may be offered to members of a family office but also the services delivered. But like all ventures that break new ground, this one gives rise to questions and poses challenges that call for creative solutions. Here are a few of the issues that have been raised so far and how we plan to address them.

Problem: How can we build The Cabin without money? How can we raise money from members before there is a liquidity event? Once the liquidity event has taken place, how can we, in good conscience, ask client members to write the big checks to fund The Cabin's development even as we're telling them to hold off on making unnecessary decisions during their time in the DFZ?

Answer: We can't, and we wouldn't.

Solution: Invite certain shareholders to join The Cabin now by transferring some shares of Northville to The Cabin before the liquidity event so that when there is liquidity, the funds will be available right away and The Cabin can be built.

Problem: How can we manage to get hundreds of Northville shareholders to pledge a percentage of their shares in advance of a liquidity event? Even if we could get more than a hundred pledges, how could we hire people, build all the departments, and provide the members meaningful wealth-coaching services within a reasonable period of time?

Answer: We can't and we can't.

Solution: Start with a manageable number of Northville shareholders who have a large number of shares and likely need more immediate assistance than smaller shareholders. Invite them to be among the founding families of The Cabin by transferring a small percentage of their shares to The Cabin in advance of the liquidity event.

Problem: The Cabin is just a concept at this stage, not a legal entity. How can founding families transfer Northville shares to an entity that doesn't exist?

Answer: They can't.

Solution: Form a legal entity for The Cabin.

Problem: We have no control over when or even if there will be a liquidity event. At this stage, how can we know what type of legal entity to form (be it LLC, C corp, S corp, etc.), and even if we did, why would we want to manage and administrate that entity before it has a purpose?

Answer: We can't know and we wouldn't want to manage it yet.

Solution: Invite the founding family members to pledge, via a letter of intent, to prepay The Cabin membership dues by transferring a small percentage of their Northville shares to The Cabin after a legal entity is formed but before the liquidity event.

And that's exactly what we did. This is the generic version of the letter of invitation we used:

> I, SHAREHOLDER NAME, am an investor in Northville, Inc. It is anticipated that at some time my investment will result in a significant liquidity event (or series of events). I understand that when this event happens, I will be in a new-to-me economic position and I will want assistance to manage and enjoy the changes I will experience.
>
> The purpose of this letter-of-intent is to agree to participate as a founding member in The Cabin. To date, The Cabin is a concept and not a legal entity. The Cabin does not plan to create a legal

structure until there is evidence a liquidity event is imminent. The purpose of waiting to form a legal structure is to minimize administrative, legal, and accounting requirements before they are necessary and recognize that it is possible the structure may never be necessary. Delaying the formation of a legal structure will also provide maximum flexibility.

Even though The Cabin is merely an idea, it is a well-thought-out idea that has been vetted by Paul Gideon, George Berman, Myra Salzer, and numerous advisors and consultants since work on it began in the spring of 2010. The Cabin's purpose is to provide a safe haven for investors, who will be selectively invited to join over time. In many cases, we anticipate it will take at least five years before we can provide services to all shareholders in our circle.

I am being invited to join The Cabin as a founding member. As a founding member, I will participate in The Cabin's creation and build out from the start. I will be invited to participate in the services shown in the attached diagram (The Cabin Structure) as they become available. I recognize the build-out of The Cabin will likely take several years.

It is my understanding that The Cabin will be a service organization whose legal structure will be for profit (for tax purposes) and whose intention will be to collect revenue through membership dues that will closely track expenses for the services being provided. Membership dues will be charged pro rata, based on services provided. As a founding member, initial dues will be a flat x-tenths of one percent (0.x%) of the shares I control for myself, in trust, or other legal entity(ies). Based on the financial projections presented to me, this initial fee of 0.x% of my shares is anticipated to provide The Cabin with the liquidity it will need in the first year to 18 months, depending on Northville, Inc.'s payout and The Cabin's build-out rates.

I understand my initial deposit will not be refundable, even if I decide not to become a founding member after transferring my shares. I also understand this is a nonbinding letter of intent and the nonrefundability component of this agreement will take effect upon transfer of the shares into The Cabin's legal entity. Though I recognize I can leave The Cabin at any time, I am accepting this invitation to become a founding member with the intention of it being the first step in a lifetime of working with The Cabin, in whatever form it ultimately takes.

By signing below, I am formalizing my intention to become a founding member of The Cabin.

Founding Member Signature ————————————————

Date ————————————————————————

It was easy to decide who the founding family invitees should be. Paul knows most of the shareholders. The eight largest shareholder families represent more than 57 percent of the total shares among the group. Fortunately, all eight were aligned with regard to values and ethics. Without question, they would be invited to be among the founding families.

Eight additional shareholders were invited. Except for me, each did have a sizeable number of shares but not anywhere near as many as the first eight shareholders. They did, however, offer expertise and/or connections that will help with the build-out.

One by one, Paul and I (and sometimes George) will have met with each invitee, face to face, to present the letter of invitation, the diagrams of The Cabin's Structure and Experience, and Paul's expertly prepared financial projections that supported the initial funding percentage of shares. At the time of this writing, each founding family member we approached has committed to this letter of invitation.

Once we have reason to believe Northville is within six months of making a distribution to shareholders, we will work with general counsel to form a legal entity for The Cabin. Once it's formed, we will request the pledged shares from the founding family members. Simultaneously, we'll begin our search for a chief operating officer and recruit the wisdom counsel and international investment counsel, Sara Hamilton and Charlie Grace, from The Family Office Exchange, and lean hard on Jim Grubman, Ph.D. and Susan Bradley. That's when the real work begins—and when the real fun starts.

The Challenges and the Rewards

For me, designing The Cabin has been an interesting balancing act. I'm not in a position to assess the viability of Northville's technology. I have no way to assess Paul's and George's ability to do so either. Yet I have invested hundreds of hours and thousands of dollars in the creation of an entity that may never come to fruition, for a group of individuals with whom I would otherwise have little connection.

I have a family and I have a business, so time spent on The Cabin has meant less time for them. My family and colleagues have been over-the-top supportive. Ten years ago, I envisioned having time to learn piano and Spanish after coming home and walking the dog. Such leisurely pursuits seem almost laughable now. Thanks to my capable coworkers, TWC has continued to grow and thrive in spite of my divided attention. My loyal, wonderful husband picked up the slack at home. How did I get so lucky?

Sometimes I think that not knowing what the ultimate outcome will be for Northville is a blessing because I'll be free to continue to build on the amazing contacts I've established and the friends I've made. My greatest **concern** is that we eventually find out there isn't going to be a liquidity event and I will lose the credibility I spent a lifetime building. My second-greatest concern is that the liquidity event turns out to be all that we've planned for.

Either way, it will be fascinating.

CHAPTER NINE

It Takes a Village

• • •

Designing something as complex and innovative as The Cabin is inspiring and tremendously satisfying, but tackling the many questions triggered by its design can also be intimidating. When you're in uncharted territory, you can't rely solely on instincts and experience to get you where you want to go. You need someone to point the way—especially someone whose experience and wisdom can shed light on the more puzzling questions that arise.

In designing The Cabin, I've been enlightened and informed by many people, but there's one in particular whose help and guidance have been invaluable—Jay Hughes. His help has continued as we've worked on The Cabin, a vision he calls "noble and very impressive."

Almost invariably, he'd raise an issue we hadn't considered. During one meeting with Jay in Denver as we shared a drink before dinner, he pulled out a napkin that looked as though he'd been scribbling on it for weeks. He started off by calling me the CEO of the project. Hold on, I said. We were thinking it would be a good idea *not* to have a CEO. The idea was to have an organization without a hierarchy, where people lead themselves, and everyone pitches in. Jay listened then, in that Zen-like way he has, pointed out that my ideal vision of governance would inevitably have a head-on collision with reality. It needed to be rethought—and the sooner the better—unless I wanted to risk having The Cabin blow up on takeoff.

The napkin outlined some essential "counsels" that would be needed: a wisdom counsel (and he listed nine colleagues whom he recommended), a legal counsel, a chief counsel, an in-house philosopher (how many family-office philosophers have you met?), and a counsel for dynamic preservation (that is, an investment counsel). He also said The Cabin would need a chief operating officer (he had a couple names for me to consider) and a CFO. The need for these two was obvious to me, until I realized that Jay's definition of CFO wasn't chief financial officer but rather chief *fiduciary* officer. Once again, I realized that when it came to understanding the help we would need, Jay understood The Cabin completely.

Jay called me an elder. *Who, me? I'm just a beginner,* I thought. But Jay's confidence in me gave me confidence in myself. Nothing like The Cabin had ever been conceived. Jay got it! He had confidence in my ability to pull it off, and he volunteered to guide us. He agreed to join regular Skype meetings with George, Paul, and me. The meetings were about a month apart for the first several months and later were held as needed and if available. Jay was remarkably available, despite his travels.

Between meetings, we had homework assignments. We usually accomplished all we set out to do, in spite of Jay's inability to be truly retired, the demands of my work at The Wealth Conservancy,

Paul's work at his other companies, and George's ventures. We made quite a team.

My Many Mentors

Looking back, I cannot believe our luck. There are so many amazing people who have come together, who've risen to the challenge, who've offered their help, their time, and their wisdom, even when they were skeptical about the viability of Northville and its technology. They aren't yellow-page pros; they're professionals at the top of their field. Some, like Sara Hamilton and Charlotte Beyer, created a field and forum that otherwise wouldn't exist. Others influenced me personally. Many of the people listed below, either named or anonymous, made a direct contribution. Undoubtedly, I have overlooked some contributors. Please accept my humble apology.

Sara Hamilton and Charlie Grace of Family Office Exchange (FOX, foxexchange.com) are based in Chicago and New York. Just as The Cabin is nothing more than a concept and a vision, Sara created FOX on little more than that. Now it's the world's best known clearinghouse for family offices. Charlie Grace, after serving in his own family office, is a senior consultant at FOX. These two knowledgeable "class acts" spent a whole day with Paul, George, and me to brainstorm the concept of The Cabin. They brought decades of experience, knowledge, and expertise to the challenge, at no charge, just for the fun of co-creating it and for the satisfaction of making a contribution. Sara knew little about me, since I've never worked with family offices, and Charlie had never heard of me. George and Paul were unknown to both of them as well. Though we were literally pro bono handouts with nothing more than a dream to offer, we'll avoid hundreds of mistakes because of the benefit of their advice. They're among the first people we'll call when we can afford what they're worth.

Dan Sullivan doesn't even know what The Cabin is. I've never discussed it with him. But Dan has been my entrepreneurial coach since the 1990s. He and his wife, Babs Smith, have been my inspiration ever since I met them. Their firm, Strategic Coach (strategiccoach.com), is dedicated to coaching successful entrepreneurs who want to achieve even greater success, and I dutifully and eagerly attend quarterly meetings in Chicago for my ninety-day fix of focus and energy. The Wealth Conservancy and I wouldn't be where we are today without the benefit of Dan as my coach, not to mention the examples Dan and Babs set. They've built a multi-million-dollar, international firm with more than a hundred employees and more than twenty independent-contract coaches. Dan has developed practice-management tools that I use daily, and slowly but surely, I'm mastering the concepts he has introduced me to. Though he might not approve of the "not intended to make a profit" concept, I am confident that he would support our vision of a well-run, fun, energetic, and service-oriented firm with hundreds of employees being given permission to be "intrapreneurs."

Kristin Keffeler is an industry up-and-comer, and we are lucky to have her in our corner. Based in Niwot, near Boulder, she consults with family offices and inheritors. Because of her background in business and leadership coaching, along with her personal experience as a child of a successful entrepreneur, she "gets it." Already, she has offered The Wealth Conservancy's employees one of her educational sessions about managing change, a subject near and dear to everyone associated with The Cabin. Kristin educated us about understanding the dynamics of change and navigating the chaos it brings. We anticipate this will be a necessary skill for all client members and The Cabin staff.

A world-renown but anonymous general counsel team came to our aid during the first couple years of developing our concept.

One of the terms of our agreement was that they would remain anonymous. We spent more time coming to agreement than we did consulting with them. In the process, we also learned more about how we might work together in the future. In a nutshell, we agreed to pay a fraction of their normal hourly rate for the work they did for us between the time we signed the agreement and July 2012. George, Paul, and I were so respectful of their generosity that we hardly took advantage of the offer. They were so fair in their billing practices that the balance due upon the liquidity event will be less than one percent of what we originally budgeted. But in that short time, we learned many valuable strategies.

Were it not for a shareholder I'll call Kindra—a name that captures what I feel is our kindred, spiritual connection—Paul wouldn't have found out about Northville. He wouldn't have told George, nor would he have spoken to the others who later became investors. Kindra is profoundly special. Her corporate and business background doesn't interfere with her understanding of the good Northville can offer the world. She connected with the lead scientist and founder of Northville and recognized the truth of the technology. She saw what it could mean to the planet and poured her heart and soul into making it happen while sacrificing her own time, energy, and finances along the way. She supported Paul, George, and me as we created The Cabin, having no interest in becoming a participating member. I feel deeply indebted to Kindra and would love to give back if she ever decides to take advantage of any or all of the services The Cabin will offer.

Mark Sather, attorney-at-law, has been TWC's corporate attorney for years. He not only guides me personally but also reviews legal—mainly estate-planning documents—for the firm's clients. Over the years, he's also become a friend. After sharing one of the initial diagrams for The Cabin with Mark, I was heartened to hear he had an interest in working on the philanthropy side. In the interim, he's donated much time and legal know-how to The Cabin.

Similarly, Bill Cline, CPA, is an accountant for several of The Wealth Conservancy's clients and staff members. His background includes providing family-office services at a New York firm, so he knows what's involved and is interested in heading and staffing The Cabin's Accounting Department.

The great Susan Bradley, author of *Sudden Money*, founder of The Sudden Money Institute (Suddenmoney.com), and all-around wonderful person, is an expert on teaching financial planners how to work with clients in transition. A transition planner understands that clients, because they're simultaneously experiencing *and* trying to plan for a big change, often do not have the know-how needed to navigate the change. Susan recognizes the need for a "decisions-free-zone" (DFZ) to give clients permission to hold off on making unnecessary decisions while they're "impaired," that is, overwhelmed with change and unable to make wise decisions. She coaches planners on how to hone in on the important issues that require decisions and put off those that are not urgent. She and psychologist Jim Grubman, Ph.D. co-facilitated a presentation for shareholders at Paul's house in September 2012 to explain what they might experience upon the liquidity event. This presentation was a direct result of Paul's commitment to providing education to client members. We hope that Susan will head The Cabin's wealth-coaching department when the time is right.

The capable and affable Jim Grubman, Ph.D. (JamesGrubman. com) practices in Massachusetts. His clients are families of wealth, inheritors, wealth creators, and the financial-planning firms that serve these clients. Jim has studied the effects of wealth on each of these types of clients and has written many articles on the topic as well as a book, *Strangers In Paradise*. In his presentation during the session Susan offered on coping with change, he drew an analogy between "immigrant" wealth creators and "native" inheritors. I imagine the analogy helped shareholders understand what to expect and how change will affect who they are after a liquidity event occurs. Jim will head the Counseling Department at The Cabin. Though our Northville shareholders are generally in good emotional health, the magnitude of the disruption caused by the liquidity event could result in a significant need for Jim's services. He is anticipating that need and preparing for it.

Many others have made contributions, either directly or via their influence. They include Charlotte Beyer (founder of the Institute for Private Investors), John A. Warnick (estate attorney and founder of the Purposeful Planning Collaboration), Roy Ballentine (financial planner extraordinaire and founder, CEO of Ballentine Partners), Kathy Wiseman (founder of Working Systems, Inc.), Steve Henningsen and the entire staff at TWC, Nancy Kline, Bryan Dunn, Domingo Such III, Jim Duggan (attorney), Judith Glaser (author and founder of Communications, Inc.), Grady Boles (financial planner), and Courtney Pullen (consultant to families and financial-profession firms and founder of Pullen Consulting), to name a few.

Mark Sather helped Paul design participation agreements for some of the professionals who continue to donate their time and wisdom. We intend to compensate everyone, and for those who are investing large amounts of time, we put that intention in writing.

Only three people declined our invitation to come on board after we shared our vision. All three were candidates for chief operating officer. We flew one of them into Boulder, and it was obvious that there was no heart connection. He knew his nuts and bolts (a prerequisite for a possible COO), but he didn't get us. Another disconnect was with an attorney that George, Paul, Kindra, and I drove hours to meet. He also knew his stuff and is a leader in his field. In fact, he's so well known nationally in a very specialized field, that I can't mention his area of expertise. Another prospective COO we talked with invested a good amount of time learning about us. We wanted him. We still do. He would be great. But he never made it to Boulder to experience our culture because he was quite certain that the position would not have given him enough face time with members. He described himself as an *onmivert*, one who needs both isolation and connection. I loved that he knew that about himself, and I wish I could have shown him how the vision I have for the COO position would be perfect for an onmivert.

So, as we go to press, we still do not have a COO candidate, but we're open to nominations.

Before entering the financial services industry, Myra earned a Bachelor of Science degree in chemical engineering at Case Western Reserve University and worked for major corporations in that field. In 1983, she transitioned away from engineering and became a CERTIFIED FINANCIAL PLANNER™ professional. She is founder and president of The Wealth Conservancy, Inc., in Boulder, Colorado, where she and her colleagues provide wealth-coaching and financial-planning services to clients nationwide.

She frequently speaks and publishes on financial issues, and Worth magazine has chosen her multiple times as one of the nation's top financial advisors. She prefers advocating for and empowering those who have inherited significant assets and want to harness their wealth's potential and focus on their life's greatest ambitions.

Salzer and her husband have two grown daughters and live with their dog in the foothills just outside of Boulder.

Index

Made in the USA
Lexington, KY
04 July 2018